Marie Curie

A Photo-Illustrated Biography
by Greg Linder

Consultant:
Mary Victoria Frohne, Ph.D.
Assistant Professor of Physics
Western Illinois University

Bridgestone Books
an imprint of Capstone Press
Mankato, Minnesota

Bridgestone Books are published by Capstone Press
818 North Willow Street, Mankato, Minnesota 56001
http://www.capstone-press.com

Library of Congress Cataloging-in-Publication Data
Linder, Greg, 1950–
    Marie Curie: a photo-illustrated biography/by Greg Linder.
    p. cm.—(Photo-illustrated biographies)
    Includes bibliographical references and index.
    Summary: A biography of the scientist who discovered radium and won two Nobel Prizes.
    ISBN 0-7368-0206-1
    1. Curie, Marie, 1867–1934—Juvenile literature. 2. Chemists—Poland—Biography—Juvenile
literature. [1. Curie, Marie, 1867–1934. 2. Chemists. 3. Women—Biography] I. Title. II. Series.
QD22.C8L56 1999
540'.92—dc21
[B]
                                                                            98-46104
                                                                               CIP
                                                                                AC

Editorial Credits
Chuck Miller, editor; Timothy Halldin, cover designer; Kimberly Danger, photo researcher

Photo Credits
Corbis-Bettmann, cover, 4, 6, 8, 10, 12, 16, 18, 20; Corbis-Bettmann/The Mariners' Museum, 14

Table of Contents

Matter and Energy

Marie Curie was one of the world's most famous physicists. Her study of matter and energy led her to discover radium.

Most physicists thought atoms were the smallest particles of matter. But in 1898, Marie discovered that radium atoms are unstable. They break apart into smaller particles that have a lot of energy. These particles are called radiation. Marie's discovery led to the treatment of cancer with radioactivity. Cancer is a disease that destroys healthy cells in the body.

Marie's husband, Pierre, also was a physicist. He and Marie studied radioactivity together. In 1903, they received a Nobel Prize in physics. This prize recognizes people whose work benefits humanity.

In 1911, Marie received a second Nobel Prize. This time, she won it in the field of chemistry. She was the first person to receive two Nobel Prizes.

Marie believed atoms were not the smallest particles of matter. This belief led to the discovery of radium and its uses.

Childhood in Poland

Maria Sklodowska was born November 7, 1867, in Warsaw, Poland. She later changed her first name to Marie. She was the youngest of five children.

Marie's mother, Bronislawa, was a school principal. She left her job after Marie was born.

Marie's father, Vladislav, was a professor of physics and math. He taught at a high school in Warsaw. Marie's father taught her to love science.

In the 1860s, Russia ruled Poland. Government officials took jobs from Poles and gave them to Russians. Vladislav lost many jobs. The family had to manage money wisely. They rented rooms in their home to university students.

Bronislawa died from a lung disease called tuberculosis in 1878. But Bronislawa had taught Marie and the other children to survive. Marie taught and cared for children to help her family earn money.

Marie (left) gave some money she earned to her sister Bronya. The money helped send Bronya to school to become a doctor.

"I like school. Perhaps you will make fun of me, but nevertheless, I must tell you that I like it, and even that I love it."
—Marie as a teenager in a letter to her best friend

Becoming a Scientist

Marie graduated from high school when she was 15. She earned the highest grades in her class. Marie wanted to continue her education. But girls were not allowed to attend universities in Poland. Marie worked as a teacher and caretaker for children.

In 1891, Marie moved to Paris, France. She studied science at a famous university called the Sorbonne (sor-BAHN).

Marie had learned to read French in Poland. But she had trouble understanding her professors at the Sorbonne. They spoke quickly and used difficult words. Marie spent every spare moment studying.

In 1893, Marie's hard work led to a degree in physics. In 1894, she earned a degree in mathematics.

Marie now wanted to study the magnetic properties of metals. But she needed a laboratory where she could work on her experiments.

Marie lived with Bronya while attending the Sorbonne. Bronya was now a doctor in Paris and helped pay for Marie's schooling.

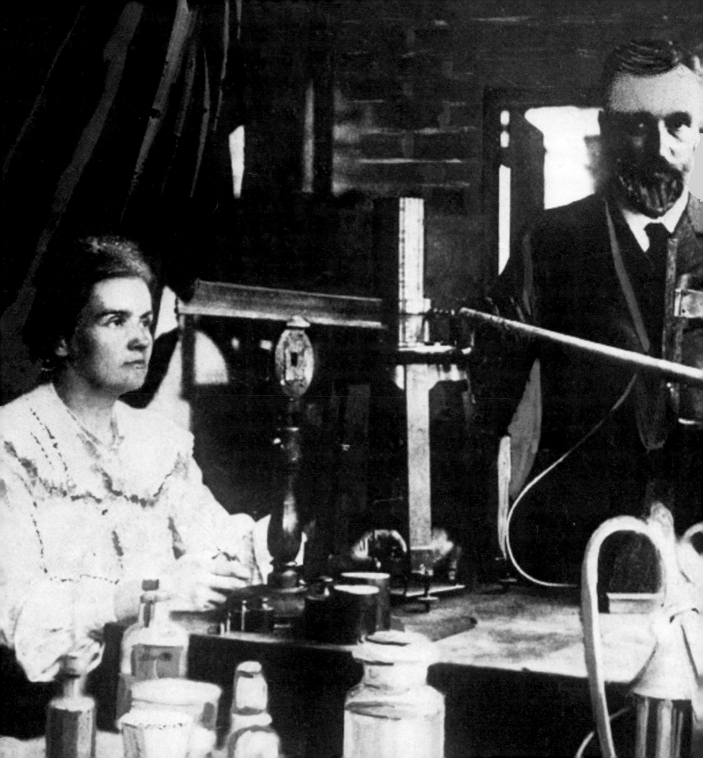

Marie and Pierre

Pierre Curie was 35 years old when he met Marie. Pierre was a respected physicist. He was well-known for his work with quartz crystals. He had learned that squeezing these colorless rocks creates electricity.

Pierre offered Marie laboratory space in Paris. She began working alongside him. Pierre had never met a woman who was so serious about science. He soon asked Marie to marry him. Pierre and Marie married on July 26, 1895.

Marie decided to return to the Sorbonne after the wedding. She wanted to earn a doctorate. This is the highest degree offered by a university. No woman in Europe had ever received a doctorate.

To earn her doctorate, Marie had to conduct a scientific study. She chose to study uranium. Scientists knew this metal contains a lot of energy. Marie wanted to know more about the energy.

Marie and Pierre spent much of their time in the laboratory. But the couple also had two daughters, Eve and Irène.

Discovery of Radium

Marie had studied atoms at the Sorbonne earlier. Scientists believed there was no smaller particle of matter than the atom. But Marie thought atoms might be made of smaller parts. She thought the energy in uranium came from parts inside the atoms. She was right. Her idea later changed the study of physics.

Marie began to study rock samples. She tested a uranium ore called pitchblende. This metal had more energy than uranium. Marie decided pitchblende must contain a new element. She was determined to find it.

In 1898, Pierre stopped his experiments. He joined Marie in her search for the new element. Marie and Pierre worked with many tons of pitchblende.

In December, Marie and Pierre told scientists they had discovered radium. This element was two million times more radioactive than uranium.

Marie worked to find and create new radioactive elements. Pierre studied how the elements affected people and the environment.

"Radium ought not to enrich anyone.
It is an element. It belongs to everybody."
–Marie explaining to a journalist why
she did not make money from radium

Fame and Success

For the next four years, Marie and Pierre studied radium and radiation. Pierre and others discovered that radiation can destroy cancerous tissue. Doctors began using radium to treat cancer patients. Marie and Pierre became famous for discovering this amazing element. They had the opportunity to sell radium and become rich. Instead, they explained to other scientists how to make and use radium.

Marie received her doctorate in 1903. Marie and Pierre received a greater honor that year. They were awarded the Nobel Prize in physics. This award is the highest honor a scientist can receive.

In 1904, Pierre became the head professor of physics at the Sorbonne. University officials promised to build him a new laboratory. Marie would be in charge of the new laboratory.

Marie became an instant celebrity when she discovered radium.

Working Alone

Today, people know that too much radiation can be harmful. But radiation was a new science in the early 1900s. Marie and Pierre thought little about working with radioactive elements.

Both Marie and Pierre started to show signs of sickness. Marie's fingers were burned and cracked. Pierre had terrible pains in his legs. Marie feared he would die from his illness.

But Pierre's illness did not kill him. On April 19, 1906, a horse-drawn carriage hit him. Pierre was killed instantly.

Marie took Pierre's place at the Sorbonne. She was the first woman to teach there.

In 1909, Marie created a sample of pure radium. In 1911, Marie received a Nobel Prize in chemistry for this creation. She was the first person to win two Nobel Prizes.

Marie won her two Nobel Prizes in different scientific areas. The first was for physics. The second was for chemistry.

Saving Lives

The Radium Institute opened at the Sorbonne on July 31, 1914. Scientists and students at this large laboratory studied radioactivity. Marie became the new institute's director.

Two days later, the German army attacked France. This attack marked the beginning of France's entry into World War I (1914–1918). Work stopped at the Radium Institute.

Marie wanted to help France. She decided to bring x-ray machines to battlefields. The machines took pictures of the inside of soldiers' bodies. The pictures showed bullets, broken bones, and other problems. Doctors then could treat the soldiers.

Marie and her daughter Irène learned how to operate x-ray machines. Marie and Irène also trained 150 women to take x-rays. The women x-rayed about 1 million soldiers during the war.

Irène also was interested in radioactivity. Irène won the Nobel Prize in chemistry for discovering a new way of creating radiation.

"I am among those who think science has great beauty. A scientist in a laboratory is not only a technician; he is also a child placed before natural phenomena which impress him with all the wonder of a fairy tale."
–Marie speaking to the League of Nations, 1933

Final Years

The Radium Institute reopened in 1920. But scientists there had no radium to study. At the time, radium was more expensive than gold.

Women in the United States read about the institute's problem. They raised $150,000 for Marie. Marie traveled to the United States in 1921. President Warren G. Harding gave her a golden key. The key unlocked a case that held one gram of radium. The women's money had paid for the radium.

In 1934, Marie's health became worse. She died on July 4 at age 66. Marie died of a form of cancer called leukemia. Leukemia affects the body's blood cells. Scientists believe too much radiation caused Marie's illness.

Marie's discoveries saved the lives of many people. Her ideas helped scientists understand parts of atoms they never knew existed.

Marie accepted a donation of radium from President Harding in 1921. The radium allowed her to continue her work until her death.

Fast Facts about Marie Curie

 Marie discovered the radioactive element polonium. It was named after her birthplace of Poland.

 Irène Curie won the Nobel Prize in chemistry in 1935. Marie and Irène are the only mother and daughter to win the prize.

 Marie received 15 gold medals, 19 degrees, and many other honors for her work as a physicist.

Important Dates in Marie Curie's Life

1867—Born November 7, in Warsaw, Poland

1891—Moves to Paris and begins to study at the Sorbonne

1895—Marries Pierre Curie on July 26

1898—Discovers radium

1903—Awarded the Nobel Prize in physics

1906—Pierre dies; Marie begins to teach physics at the Sorbonne

1909—Becomes first person to create a sample of pure radium

1911—Awarded the Nobel Prize in chemistry

1914—Becomes director of the new Radium Institute

1934—Dies from leukemia on July 4

Words to Know

cancer (KAN-sur)—a disease that destroys healthy cells in the body
laboratory (LAB-ruh-tor-ee)—a place where scientists perform experiments to learn new things
leukemia (loo-KEE-mee-uh)—a form of cancer that affects blood cells
Nobel Prize (noh-BELL PRIZE)—an award given to scientists and others whose work benefits humanity; the Nobel Prize is the highest award a scientist can receive.
physicist (FIZ-uh-sist)—a person who studies matter and energy
radioactivity (ray-dee-oh-ak-TIV-uh-tee)—a process in which atoms break apart and create a lot of energy
x-ray machine (EKS-ray muh-SHEEN)—a machine that takes pictures of the inside of the human body

Read More

Fisher, Leonard Everett. *Marie Curie.* New York: Macmillan Publishing Company, 1994.
Pflaum, Rosalynd. *Marie Curie and Her Daughter Irène.* Minneapolis: Lerner Publications, 1993.
Poynter, Margaret. *Marie Curie: Discoverer of Radium.* Great Minds of Science. Hillside, N.J.: Enslow Publishers, 1994.

Useful Addresses

Center for the History of Physics
American Institute of Physics
1 Physics Ellipse
College Park, MD 20740

French Embassy in Canada
Scientific Department
464 Wilbrod Street
Ottawa, ON K1N 6M8
Canada

Internet Sites

Marie Curie
http://www.gale.com/gale/cwh/curiem.html
Science Hero—Marie Curie
http://myhero.com/science/curie.asp
Science in Poland—Marie Sklodowska-Curie
http://hum.amu.edu.pl/~zbzw/ph/sci/msc.htm

Index